Our Emotions Get Carried Away Beyond Us

Danielle Cadena Deulen

Our Emotions Get Carried Away Beyond Us

Danielle Cadena Deulen

Barrow Street Press
New York City

Designed by Robert Drummond
Cover image by Paul X Rutz

Published 2015 by Barrow Street, Inc., a not-for-profit
(501) (c) 3) corporation. All contributions are tax deductible.
Distributed by:
Barrow Street Books
P.O. Box 1558
Kingston, RI 02881

Barrow Street Books are also distributed by Small Press
Distribution, SPD, 1341 Seventh Street Berkeley, CA 94710-1409,
spd@spdbooks.org; (510) 524-1668, (800) 869-7553 (Toll-free within
the US); amazon.com; Ingram Periodicals Inc., 1240 Heil Quaker
Blvd, PO Box 7000, La Vergne TN 37086-700 (615) 213-3574; and
Armadillo & Co., 7310 S. La Cienega Blvd, Inglewood, CA 90302,
(310) 693-6061.

Special thanks to the University of Rhode Island English
Department and especially the PhD Program in English, 60 Upper
College Road, Swan 114, Kingston, RI 02881, (401) 874-5931, which
provides valuable in-kind support, including graduate and
undergraduate interns.

First Edition

Library of Congress Control Number: 2015950216

ISBN 978-0-9893296-7-5

For Max

CONTENTS

Notes

Aknowledgements

"We are never 'at home': we are always outside ourselves. Fear, desire, hope impel us toward the future; they rob us of feelings and concern for what now is, in order to spend time over what will be—even when we ourselves shall be no more."

from "Our Emotions Get Carried Away Beyond Us"
Michel de Montaigne

Burning House

Because the place was long abandoned, rumored
haunted, and because they all stood at the threshold
between winter and spring, some mornings
almost warm, or at least backlit in yellow light

the color of the sunflower fields that would,
any day now, rise up, shake the snowdrifts from their
thin shoulders, it was cause more for celebration
than alarm. No one knew how the first flame caught—

the spontaneous combustion of old newspapers,
perhaps, or a pinpoint light burned into the arm
of an antique chair, some late beauty waiting
to burn again, or the air oiled by a broken gas line

sparked by a rogue wire in the haggard walls.
When the fire truck's siren sounded, lightning-voiced
through the street, the people stumbled out, blinking their eyes,
brought thermoses and bundled babies who pointed

toward the flames. And they nodded, *Yes, Yes—Fire,*
to the babies, to each other, smiling into the glitter-
rush melting away the snow, the water-stream rising
into a fine cloud of vapor above the ruin, above

the children dancing up to touch the cold water, delighted
by the sudden arrival of heat, their gray days turned
August. Soon, they knew, soon, they would run out into
those snow-pressed fields beyond the flames, hunch down

in the brush to hide from each other, to strike the matches
they stole from their mothers' purses to make small fires
from tinder, matted feathers, the dried bodies of crickets,
small as secrets, let them burn in the palms of their hands.

We Can Savor Nothing Pure

Begin from this moment and go back rapidly in time, as you would in a film, until you reach the sound of cave-wind. Perfect darkness. The ancestor utterly naked, rock damp beneath her bare feet and a loose bundle of tinder in her palm: dried grass, shavings from the inner bark of cottonwood (which burns even when wet), matted hair, windblown seed. She is there.

Or she is not there. She stands there, or her lithe, filthy body, her wild hair, is just another image in a succession of images arranged (by whom?) for heightened romantic aura. For the Romance of the Self. Not the self beneath fluorescent lights. Not the self devouring processed meat in a nearly empty parking lot contemplating the cut at the tip of the finger and the impossibility

of unselfish kindness. Not the self on a slow drive to the office, past ailing strip malls and unconscious men pissing themselves beneath bus stop awnings. The self as it can only exist in imagination, the pure self by which we measure and resent the actual. Outside, nothing is yet invented. Wind in the trees and wind in the cave. No longing more complicated than hunger or

sex. Wind in the cave of the mind. She drops a glowing coal into the tinder nest, lifts it in her cupped hands, lightly blows until it catches fire. The heat of it in her palms. The way the air seems to open, the darkness suddenly alive, the shadows trying to tell a story. Pigment on stone. The figures are trying to tell you a story. They are trying to tell you a story

or they aren't. The problem of knowing the story is that we think that knowing means we know its purpose. Because pleasure is never purpose enough. Because it must be measured, kept, diagrammed as in the textbook forms of anatomy. Because when they finally mapped the internal structure of the clitoris, they found an organ of vast elegance curving through the pelvis near

the base of the spine, and were surprised—they found an electric shock, the hot brain a constellation of nerves suddenly burning too bright, and yet brighter, so bright they burned themselves out, becoming part of the darkness that once surrounded them. A deep darkness. A cave. As it was in the beginning, when a voice sang darkness into the light to make the light bearable.

Later, another voice called the dark wicked—the moon, a totem in a devil's mouth. At that moment everyone was lying in the hills— lying in the hills, staring up at the stars, not wishing for daylight or sleep. *Be careful,* the voice said, *pleasure will surely kill us,* and kept saying it until it seemed to come from no one—wind in the cave of the mind—until everyone stood up

and walked home, not touching, not looking into each other's faces, or stretching their arms up into the silver light. And later, when they heard the far-off buzz of locusts flying toward their fields, they were certain it was a warning—that it must be the sound of the wailing ghosts of the first people to hear music, who fell so in love with song they starved.

Dirge with a Love Song in it

An ache at the back of my skull and the snow-
dredged distance seem

to coincide, as do the abdicating boughs
of dogwood and the lone girl in her

woolen coat, who waits at the corner for the light
to change. It's the lack

of color in her cheeks. No—it's the way she clasps
her hands—a falling prayer—how the windows

of the office building across the street divide her
reflection with their grid of blinds—the way

the workers leave exactly as the moon rises,
a burning memory above them in the worn

kettle of the night—how they've become the thin
broth they might have sipped as fevered children—

that reminds me of you, the you I've only seen
in black-and-white, your skinny legs

and large dark eyes, your serious mouth pressed shut

as mine is now. I'm driving. The road is a pattern
in your funeral dress—swirling and smooth—the ash

of your hands quietly folded. The priest in my mind
murmurs something about the body—how vulnerable

the body, like warm wax. I'm too far away to hear.
A love song swoons on the radio, like one

you must have heard on your drive (sixty-five years ago)
to L.A. from Tuscon where you left behind

a husband still laughing at the bruise he left on your cheek,
the baby asleep in the backseat. You glanced

in the rearview, then at your own face in the mirror, the dry
black road shimmering like a wake. I am ashamed to say

I never thanked you for driving toward a future
into which I would someday be born. The radio plays

and I turn it up, a bridge blaring like the slow
explosions that fill my dreams: I run and run and turn

the corner of an unfamiliar hallway, an unclasped door
opening to an aisle. See how light enters the dirge,

the stillness in the field beyond the sill? See how
your family standing on the hill beneath the pine

lines up to let the loose earth slip through
their fingers back to you? See the green, sorrowed air

where I'm not, where I couldn't bear to be—
how I've driven so long thinking of you that you have

become the song, the mirror, the prayer, and the road
just past the reach of headlights.

After the Lesson

I walked home, the salt-dry snow collecting
        in the bleached scrub brush, a wide highway
                prostrate beneath the low, red sun—

a sun like a struck cymbal, echoing. I turned
        a quarter over and over in my pocket, wishing
                for a pay phone, imagining my coin

would buy a call, the way it used to in movies—
        always the phone singing and singing
                in its glass-and-metal box, lonely busker

on a corner, until someone, never the person
        the caller wanted to answer, answers. Someone
                who happened to walk by just then, amazed

by the call of the machine. A voice asks, *Hello?*
        But the receiver's already hung. Snow drifts
                into gravel at the road's shoulder, sometimes

rising up in little whirlwinds. The wind
        a dial tone—a Chopin Waltz that I didn't practice
                (I was young, I never considered my hands).

My teacher said *Again, Again,* thinking, I suppose,
        that I would eventually get it right. I heard
                someone else in the house—a son? a lover?—

clear his throat in the kitchen, lift a spoon from
        a drawer, the other silverware falling into place
                around its absence, the small twang of metal

on metal (I was young, distracted by the swirl
        of light on the keys, and I couldn't reach the chords,
                Chopin's hands so much larger than mine),

the metronome clicking away. We both knew
          I had failed. My teacher didn't even bother
                    to say it. I closed her red front door as quietly

as a score, then walked for miles along the road's
          shoulder because I hadn't prepared a way home,
                    believing home closer than it was; I was young,

I'd never thought about distance, intervals
          of time, still believing that a quarter would buy me a call,
                    that someone would answer my ringing.

What I Fear

Losing you, of course; the spider
crawling into my ear as I sleep; dementia;
the scent of lavender erased from

your body; losing your eyes closed in desire
above me as if in denial or a sight so sharp
it pains you; I don't fear death, but I fear

the pain of death; the ocean slopping around
in its huge casket; anything reaching up
through waves; knives; arthritic hands

that would strangle me; no longer hearing
your voice; no longer tasting the sweetness
of clover; coyote howl; wasp buzz; rattlesnake

on the narrow path; the white peonies I wanted
to stand for us, wilting; the mutable moon
denying she knows me; that the hand resting

at your side when you sleep will never again
find mine; I fear what steals: the proliferous
dark, beetles breeding holes in the elms, bacteria

multiplying, drought and fire, soldiers staging
themselves in the streets; I fear losing what the thief
will take away, but more that he will enter our house.

American Libretto

Hair-thin insects rise from the lawn. The basement
deepens its damp. A girl rolls her eyes,
a phone pressed between her ear and her shoulder.

In a nearby park, a crowd gathers around
a single tree. Somewhere, a faucet drips. The moon

is overemotional, waning all night. One brother
practices the same three chords on his electric-blue guitar
for hours, listening to the resonant static between frets.

One brother reads Nietzsche, considers his part in
the world's eternal recurrence. The girl rolls her eyes.

The people in the park are angry, dissatisfied
with their lives. At the roots of the tree: a dark
man curled in on himself. A boy on a bike rides slowly

past the house. He doesn't glimpse the girl inside
who has turned on her stereo to disrupt the sound

of her brother's guitar. The crowd kicks the man
as she lounges on her bed, dreaming of the boy
on her ceiling poster: skinny and tattooed, brash

purple makeup, a blonde-in-leather woman
kneeling before him. "I do not want to accuse;

I do not even want to accuse those who accuse,"
Nietzsche writes from another century. The brother
tries to imagine embracing his fate, feels it swelling

up around him like an oily tide. His father scrapes
the grill free of dried meat, preparing to roast

some other animal. Their mother is so thin that they
can hardly see her. The dark man grasps for the exposed
roots of the tree, his bloodied knuckles coated in dust.

He knows it's bad, his blood pooling before him,
made a little silver in the streetlamp. The crowd

shouts louder. Some scramble to be the first to cinch
the man's wrists with rope. The pregnant neighbor
bakes a lemon cake, humming to herself. No one knows

who the father is. A possum tries to scramble up
the aluminum trash can. The mother hears it, but just

doesn't care anymore. The brother continues to play
the same three chords to keep his hands from touching
his friend's shoulder, to keep from pressing his mouth

against his. Cicadas shimmer in the garden and the girl
rolls her eyes. Someone loops a rope around the man's

neck. He knows it's bad. It's bad. He'd speak, but
they have already shattered his mouth. The air is latent
with heat, but still cool enough for the daffodils to

slip up through it. The moon weeps over
the pregnant neighbor, staring through her window.

The boy on the bike rides slowly past the house.
On the poster, the Dream Boy has ripped the heart
out of his bandmate's chest, eyeing it as if it looks good

enough to eat. Someone throws the other end of the rope
around a branch. The mother rends the daffodils

out of their bed, walks up the stairs with them. "Looking away
shall be my only negation," one brother reads, then
turns out his light. The other brother stops playing,

but keeps the amp on to sleep to the hum of it.
Staring up at her Dream Boy, the girl thinks she'd like him

to rip out her heart, too. They've strung up the dark man,
begin charging and whipping around him, ecstatic to watch
his body twitch. Dirt falls into the eyes of the sleeping

father from the mother's trembling fistfuls, their white
sheets smeared as he turns over. The electric amp

undulates softly—rain, wind, echoes in a tunnel,
the breath of a wheel as it whirls away, a tide pulling back,
an endless exhale. In her sleep, the girl rolls her eyes.

Winter Inversion

Salt Lake City

All winter, the air has been
at record-breaking levels
of toxicity; announcers

warn not to go out in
the red days. Seagulls
displaced from coastal

cities cry *poison* over
the desert plains. We
pretend not to live

where we do, that we
don't turn away from
each other with regret.

I try to avoid breathing
in your scent. Long ago,
glaciers carved this valley,

then melted away
into sand. The change
was torture, and now

the stunned hills shudder,
go white. You see, it's not
a simple mimesis: memory

for landscape. It's the silence,
the smog, my skin blazing
for you like a lamp at the end

of a wharf where an ocean
never was, or was so long
past it no longer matters.

I can't stand it anymore.
At night, when I walk out,
I feel the crush of shells

beneath my feet—snails
fooled by the cool, wet air—
so at first I think I've arrived

at a shore, then I see how
I've murdered what would
have delighted me: how they

must have shone in the dark,
reaching out their antennae
before them, blind and gleaming.

I find no pearls within
their ruined flesh. I know
that you will never touch me.

In Movies, The Future

is always a wan dystopia, a glut
of wrong turns, buildings built
upon buildings, the wet-dark

streets trapping the hero
into unavoidable violence
and people fly, they fly

in terrible machines
as if in the guts of mantises
and no one can tell

the difference between the real
human and the one whose skin
is synthetic, whose heart

works in a low whir until
the hero stabs them and finds
instead of blood, a white froth

gushing out, and always
the androids themselves
are surprised to find they were

not, after all, human
though they had memories
felt love, were afraid

to die, believed, as we do,
that what we create we have
a right to destroy

without explanation, without
shame, which is why we share
the hero's horror at the end,

we see it in his eyes, as he slowly
stares down to his palm
cut open in the fray to find

not blood but a tangle
of wires sparking out of him,
a rush of wet white clouds.

American Curse

May dark soldiers lead you through the mountains.
May you find the criminal weeping in his hands.
May the scent of whiskey rise from your horses.
May you build your mansion in the sands.

May the beauty of your children be too great for kindness.
May the forest reappear when you close your eyes.
May your dogs grow wild as your heart goes tame.
May your bullet always meet with its aim.

On the Uncertainty of Our Judgment

Oil darkens the river upstream. Another spill, another assurance
from our mayor that the water is fine; he drinks a glass of it for the
press, their cameras swallow it up. But *purely as a precautionary
measure,* he's shut down the river water intakes, let the city draw
from its reservoirs—or someone has, some water works worker,
I imagine, in a grey jumpsuit,

two days' growth of hair on his pale face, stinking of loneliness.
Everything remains the same since Monday's spill, my breasts
leaking milk onto my sheets, onto the face of my half-lidded baby
when I jerk myself awake, asleep, awake, up on my bare feet in
the bathroom where the toilet leaks, smells faintly of piss, but in
my stupor I keep stepping into puddles,

forgetting, distracted, my baby already (I can hear him) stirring. I
turn on the faucet. Somewhere deep beneath my house, old lead
service lines pull the water up to me, where it burns over my hands.
White lead, as described in *Alexipharmaca* of Nicander: *gleaming,
deadly, whose fresh colour is like milk, which foams all over.* That
slight sting my nipples make

before the *let down* begins, but my baby is sleeping. Is he sleeping?
Maybe he's just calm, waiting to open his eyes, little planet. Last
night's storm has escaped his gaping mouth. The fists he shook at
the walls are limp now, would slip easily over the rail of his crib
like a tiny bow, rise with the music in his dreams, which swell and
turn—dark clouds beneath his lids.

No one knows how far the spill has traveled since it entered the
river, if the water has already sluiced the fuel downstream into our
pipelines. But we have assurances. *What's important here is to
recover our losses,* says the mayor, meaning *the oil*, which he has
ordered the Coast Guard to vacuum out of the water so it might
still be bought and sold. This is a value system

not much different from Greece of 15 BC, when Vitruvius wrote about the dangers of commonplace poison. He described the lead workers as having *a pallid colour; the fumes from daily casting destroyed the vigour of the blood.* But lead was abundant, malleable, with a low melting point—it was easy, everywhere. So the ancients used it to shape and solder pipes, sweeten sour wine,

line their aqueducts, transport live fish in tanks made from it, knowing its effect on the body. At this hour, there's almost silence: the metronome of the mechanical swing rocking my boy, the throated note he suckles down. Why do I imagine that water works worker to be lonely? Perhaps he's walking toward the valve intake now, imagining applause, whistling a jaunty tune,

inexplicably happy in the black morning while I hum my boy archaic lullabies, wondering if a mother's body can filter out bad water, make it sweet. I may be going mad from lack of sleep. Or perhaps it's lead in the blood—*Saturnism*, after the planet god, who orbited slowly, but erupted in violence or revelry. I'm trying to teach my son a wariness I don't abide by—the wound

just sutured shut beneath my belly where he was lifted out of me, chord noosed around his neck, into a surgical room, the lights tined around us, the silver instruments, physicians spiraling, shouting, making their assurances. When I asked what was wrong, they set my shivering newborn on my chest as if he were an answer. Should I wake him now, press

a burning nipple into his mouth, let him drain my aching breast? From outside a light brightens then seeps from his face. *It will pass*, the mayor says in every conference with the press. *It will pass*. Rising toward my son sleeping beneath the window, I feel dizzy, brace myself against the pane, my hand on the glass, wondering how hard I'd have to press to break through.

After the Revolution

it rained. Because no one had to fight any longer,
they didn't. They stood in the street,

their faces, grey from hunger, slackened a bit
around the eyes, lids fluttering in the downpour,
trying to see the point of no return

from which they had emerged victorious.
Someone tried to throw up her fist
to call out in celebration, but the rain was too heavy
and when she opened her mouth

she drowned. The others wrapped her body
in a worn tarp, naming her a martyr for the cause,
and each in their minds rang a death knell—
their skulls becoming silent bells which drew them
away, mid-ceremony, in all directions

to return to whatever they now considered home
which was, indeed, their homes before the war,
though a little dustier, a little less illusory,
and after crossing their thresholds
they went to their kitchens to boil water
for coffee or tea and once the warm liquid

had soothed their throats, they felt sleepy,
could no longer stand, stumbled into
their old bedrooms, the musk of unwashed linens
enfolding them until they sunk deep
into the trench of sleep where
each of them dreamed
different dreams.

Revision

If I could reverse it and reassemble
the cracked bodies of the crabs—their shells
no longer a lovely, silent red—restore
their frantic language of clicks and gestures
within the vast white chamber of the cooler,

sea stink settling into the fine filaments
fringing their legs, until we reach the bay
alive with dusk, the weather-worn pines
standing sentry along the shoreline, seals
with their wet-wide eyes emerging

from the currents, then submerging—
and if the tide would agree to repeat
its ebb, the sky to draw back the sun
through its arc while we all climb
again into the boat, whirl against

our wake to where we left the traps
and place each glimmering, purple crab
within the wire nets to lower them
gently into the brine, growing darker,
heavier around them until the nets nudge

their murky bed, spread wide to let them
scuttle out—if our father would steer a path
toward the harbor, let go of the throttle
so that we drift in silence until, hours
earlier, the pier appears, the morning inlet

circled by sea grass, pointed hills, the shack
where we rented our boat smelling of rinsed fish
and clay, the rough old man looking at us
like he knows as he cracks sunflower seeds
in his teeth and hands our father his change—

then I don't have to write about what
came after. We can all live here, in this day,
forward and backward, listening to
the cold-blue sea rock softly against
our metal hull, watch the gray world slowly

take on color, shadows separating
from form, the tide rushing in,
our father's real smile like a white magnolia
opening over us as we cross the bight
vibrating with light so brilliant
I have to close my eyes against it.

The End of Fathers

There, at the edge of the shore
       where there is no water,
             but a promise of water,

where the sharp moon changes
       into a full, round absence over
their shoulders as they walk, one by one,
into the sea that is
       not the sea—

And each carries a conch, the mollusk
       still at home inside, still whispering
the sounds of waves when the fathers
lift them to their ears to call, but then
       forget to call, or believe
       the number has changed, the line
       gone dead, their wives

remarried, their grown children speaking
       nakedly to their lovers at night of a heavy-worn
          memory, how colors blur
          at the edges of photographs, how faces

look different from different angles, and family resemblances
       are lost, even in the eyes and conversation
          of distant relatives. Maybe they never existed,
       as their mothers would like to believe—

The fathers can't hear it, but
       know it as they walk deeper and farther from
       the shore, the voices of their mollusks
          drying out—their steps careful into

caverns, trenches, across empty
intersections, where signals change in cycle
       without traffic. And, even if they didn't smoke before,

each father lights a cigarette to make the caverns
        seem warmer, more open—to watch the moon
        attenuate through a haze of smoke, each
                blaming another for the lack of light, the endless walk,

the way the moon turns
        away from them, and because each
is in some way a likeness of the other,
        blame themselves.

Constellation

I close my eyes and it's you with the boy
in the rain, zipping up his pants in the green,
hulking shrubs. You, marching out

like a one-girl parade, your face so white,
red-cheeked-cold and smiling like you do when
you've got away with something,

while I stand there as speechless as a crushed
bottle in the lot behind the 7-Eleven with
the other boy, waiting for you to return

and not kissing him because I've never been
kissed by anyone but you and he's not
pretty. He's smoked four Marlboros, shamed

them all beneath a rubber sole and picked at
the pimples on his chin, asking stupid
questions like *So, do you like movies?* And,

Do you think they're doing it now? As if the
thought of you unbuttoning his dirty jeans and
kneeling down in the gravel at the roots

of the bush might inspire me to prostrate
myself before him, too. You're fast.
You're so fast that almost no one can see you,

that flash across your face when your boy
doesn't stumble out declaring his love, when
we don't applaud. No one but me can see

that you think he's left you already—like your
father, your mother's boyfriend, the last boy
you kissed and the boy before him. You'll quit

school before you get through them all.
Sixteen and already a gallery of lovers: *Boy
with Car, Boy with Tattoo, Boy with Crystal*—later,

the boy who will leave money on your dresser
before he strides out your door, your face full
of sores, your teeth knocked out. He appears

behind you, encircles your waist, sucks on your
neck just to leave a mark. When we're lying,
legs tangled together later that night,

I'll touch the indefinite edges of his love-
bruise, a darkness surfacing from within your
pale skin. Of the boy, you'll say, *He says*

he thinks I'm pretty, and the stars, far up
beyond a torn screen of clouds, *They're like
diamonds in a box that no one opens.*

Lacan at the Carousel

Horses reined with iron bits in their mouths
and the golden poles through their bodies
shine silent and in mid-stride, their pink manes,

their flowered saddles, and the inanimate gaze
of their carved eyes. The center of the carousel
is ringed with mirrors to make the spectacle

of lights multiply, and the archaic music
brighter. He sits on a giraffe with his six-month-old
daughter. They go up and down in the illusion

of a gallop, though, of course, they go nowhere.
Other children squeal, but Judith is silent,
watchful the way all bastard children are.

She is constructing the memory that will
split her. Beneath the lacquered floor of the ride
is an unconscious machine, a labyrinth of gears

churning everything forward toward nothing.
At the top of the poles is consciousness.
At the root of the poles is desire. Everyone

must ride until their desire is extinguished,
or until someone intervenes. Beyond the scarlet
awning, an intricate broil of clouds, like language.

Soon, they'll all be drenched. When he pivots
to carry her off of the ride, he finds her watching
herself in the mirrors—the seams of the mirrors

interrupting her view, and she is alternately
jubilant and confused—the subject and the image,
the subject and the image. When she turns her

tea rose of a face toward him, he looks elsewhere.
In his periphery, an elephant with a rope in his teeth—
a minotaur lounging with a book—all the figures

impaled with gold, like the flash of light
from that first, ideal self—how it stabs,
repeatedly, through the center with its lie.

Transit

The horizon is doing my favorite trick:
flattening itself
                         into a blazing line. I've been watching
the sky from this plane as the plane burns

through it, the dark streaming behind—an illusion
of space and light I've stared at so long now

            I've become confused. And not a simple confusion

in which I equal the zenith of my own perspective
and you equal the burning horizon. You are
            in the horizon, and so am I.

I'm also on the plane and you are nowhere,

though several times now, I believed
            I heard your voice, turned from the window

                  to look down the aisle, as if you could possibly
                         be there. Like a dream I often had

in the years after we split—how I followed

            your echo through an apartment (that one
                  built like a thinwalled cinderblock) where
the rooms were infinite, filled
            with people I didn't know and your voice
                  steadily disappearing

into the next room. I always arrived late, just in time
to see a glimpse of your heel or elbow
                              slipping around a corner
just past a doorway,
            into nothing. I never caught you

before I awoke. Between the dream and the years
after, I began to wonder if any of it was real: you, me,
the way I could feel my pulse
                              like a moth in my throat each time
            you moved past me. When I blink

toward the aisles, I notice a circle of light obscuring
            my view (penance for staring
                              too long at the sun), a transit
in negative. Not the astral spot of Venus across

the broad hot sun, but a bright tiny form on a body
            so vast it could be the dark sky itself.
It could be the infinite, God's Love,
                              as Augustine imagined it
in a time before space
                        could be measured

before we understood everything
                              is finite, everything is
only as we perceive it. Therefore, I know that
            I loved you
                        from that knowledge alone—

though I can no longer feel that heat. Now

the dark has caught up
                        to the plane and the horizon
has burned itself out.
                        Not even the faint light
of a city below, as if we

are flying over nothing into nothing. When I rest
my temple against the glass, I swear I hear

the Atlantic shifting below
        and think of a water current in the southern hemisphere

unbroken by land that circles the earth—

        how a solitary note at certain depths will echo
           the same path endlessly—

how, if I whispered into that water, my wish would follow
        its own song of longing
           through every ocean, hypnotized

by the rhythm of waves, until someone
                    reached far enough
down to lift it into the singular air.

Elegy

The sidewalk cracks filled this morning
with ice are not widening a darkness
in me. The spirit that knocked
on my wall all night as a child, whispering
let me out, let me out, while a knot
of wire wound itself larger

and larger inside my chest, while that ice—
No. The ice has no agency. The spirit
just a rift in thought—a gap, like the gap
in the body of the raccoon I found
in a summer field—lustrous maggots shifting
together, the color of ice, of ghosts, the winter

sun melting the roads away outside. A red
bird's body blurs into some other mind. Wires
crisscross between closed houses, their white roofs
pointing toward the sky. I used to believe
the cardinal at the apex of the wooden post
outside my door could mean luck

or joy. I used to believe in an order,
in something bright but nevertheless
undetectable, like air—that it surrounded
and contained us, pensive
with its own immensity. I used to believe
in all the beauty of this world.
Now I am haunted.

To Philosophize is to Learn How to Die

That the king intends to kill Scheherazade at dusk is subtext to their romance. The scythe that met the other wives, that awaits the end of her story, shines with expectation. It listens from its casing for the king's yawn, knows how he loves a rueful death. This is why child brides are best. And this is why Scheherazade's tales are full of murder. She knows how to keep

his interest, her head. She's young enough to believe she can save the kingdom with her stories. Persian nobility took brides as young as eight years to ensure their virginity, but Scheherazade was educated, the vizier's daughter, kept from men but not from literature, science, history, art. She must have been older, more accomplished than the other thousand virgins the king had

bedded and beheaded—all merely girls. Nothing is heard of them except in the quavering voices of their parents, who begged the king to stop as they dragged their veiled daughters one by one to his bed. It's awful, yet I turn the page, read about yesterday's shooting: twenty children killed in a classroom. Each day I wake and the past remains barbarous, which is why I always wake

in mourning, which is why I can no longer take in the stories, can no longer listen. A screen flashes before me without sound or context, but I know what it means. It means nothing: an art of pure abstraction, like the works of Kandinsky and Pollock, refusing worldly resemblances. We once believed that if we knew ourselves we would perceive our faint, oil-painted glow,

but the more we looked the more we saw that everything was fractured: the odd angles of the body, the absurd faces, their uselessness, their longing to be whole. How else could anyone represent a world that could mechanize war after war, decorate and parade their murderers? The artist's eye was not a cavern into which the universe fell, it was only a reflection. And if we can never be whole, then why not be broken utterly? Call it *willful obliteration*—that's how it must have felt to the girls the king held, all pulses beneath an explosive nerve, black powder in the belly of a grenade. So, the next millennium began in blackout—now our minds can't clear the smoke, can't find an explanation for the deaths of our children,

as if their deaths weren't common, as if philosophy might soothe our grief. There is always a king and always a storyteller whose life depends on telling. What Scheherazade knew was that death is the greatest drama, and though a king appoints himself, a village lets him lead. We hold our vigils, he holds his sword. We say he is senseless as we hand him the gun. In the margins

of daylight, Scheherazade closes her eyes, sleeps tangled in silk and the shade of a tamarind tree. When she wakes, still in danger, she writes what she's dreamed. Some afternoons, when the desert wind rouses her before sunset, she goes to a stream near the palace to watch the water muddy itself and thinks of the children whose stories are silence—all along the riverbank, the reeds.

Somewhere Always Fire

That morning, explosions on the borders
east and west. I drank a lemon-mint

on a sandy balcony, the hills filled
with slender houses like books on shelves.

A piece of gravel, spun up from a passing car,
struck my eye. Then, red smoke drifted through

each scene as I saw it, as if there were, somewhere,
always fire. I called you from Amman

to hear your voice—watched vine roses spreading
like riots over the clay walls until your voice

began to sound like what I saw: brash flowers, embers,
smoking syllables. Later, I let my body float

like a corpse on the Dead Sea, a poppy blooming
from my cornea as I stared toward the shore,

a dull ache deep in my skull, a corona of light
rising from the water. *Even this close, I can't see*

what's happening, you said, when our romance began.
Your face was pressed to mine, our eyes wide

to each other. *Of course not*, I said as a winter landscape
moved across your skin—the same frozen fields

I drove through years earlier, speeding like a lost
boxcar, windows down, ice insidious on the road,

an easy slide into either lane. Something ignited
on the horizon. I knew this only because smoke

rose from it, but I couldn't see the fire, feel the fire,
or refused to, so sick I was of burning.

Why did I recall this when you pressed your mouth
to mine? How does the heart leave ash in the blood?

It's dusk now at the border as I hold out my palm.
The guard takes my history, appraises me for threat.

When he looks into to my face, I see his hesitation
as ours. In the distance, the sea is smoldering.

Sense from Sense

What began as a pearl inside her
grows into a rhythm. The fetus

strikes her belly with its mallet
heartbeat, and her once lover keeps

starting and stopping like rain.
Each morning she watches him fall short

of her threshold and begins to feel
like Descartes—wants to split sense

from sense, wants to stop the realization
of her body, his body, the body he will

leave her with. Her skin stretches taut
and she knows that what she wanted

was never possible, calls me crying,
her voice unloosed like starving cattle,

the summer done, but no one to herd them
home, dust in the river's veins. Neither

of them are in love. *Then why keep the child?*
I ask, imagining him as a conquistador,

burying his flag in her gut. But she
doesn't answer, the line plummets to

the bottom of a well-worn chasm where
two tones moan and moan but never

reach harmony. *You'll come home in August?*
she asks, adds *Otherwise, I'll be alone.*

"Alone," the connection echoes.
In summer, I'll board the plane

late, fly over the desert until I reach
the small city we grew up in. A river,

dividing dark hills from dark hills will twist
in its shallow bed, and a constellation

of streetlights on which I can divine nothing
will blink up at me like something new.

Interrogator's Love Letter

Sometimes I think I wouldn't let you leave, even if you told me everything. A map of the harbored, the coordinates of those you've loved—don't you see how it no longer matters?

Before you, I feared the intimacy of water, the way it penetrates, swells, washes away. I couldn't swim, or even stand at a shoreline without feeling rage, but now I stand for hours at the faucet, imagining your innocent mouth wetting my fingers. I rise each morning from a dream of water on your pale-skinned throat, flick open my flame for another cigarette. Humidity rises like veils over the earth and I think of the moisture in your skin.

Often, after, we pass a smoke between us, your shaking fingers touching my shaking fingers, so that your blood brightens the bleached paper before I taste it on my lips.

Tell me what I want to hear, even if it's a lie. Tell me again of the acacias, cloudlike over your childhood house, the friend you kissed in a forest of dunes—

I want you husked, burned into an

ash I could breathe. Still, I want
you to live.

Perhaps it is always like this—
driven to consume, afraid of the end
of that consummation. I burrowed
so far into you, through your derma,
your sinew, your stories, that one
morning I opened the cell and your
eyes looked like mine.

After my shock—after I knocked at
the bend of your knuckles, and after
you wept softly like rain into the red
pool you cupped in your palms, I left.

Driving toward the shore, last light
drawing back into the treacherous
hills, I found myself crying out to no
one, perhaps to you—*Now that we've
come to the end of our knowing, what
do we have left to give one another?*

But only the ocean answered,
only in waves.

Freeway

Our last fight was about a knife
he wanted just to have, he was
overly excited in the car, opened
the blade to check its gleam, not
meaning to threaten me, but I
flinched and asked him to close it
which made him angry, that I was
afraid made him angry. I heard,
but couldn't see, cars speeding past
on a nearby freeway like an ocean
in another's dream. He winnowed
the air then with the knife, slashing
toward the windshield, not exactly
in my direction, not really meaning
to threaten me, but I began to cry
and he shook his head slowly, *No*,
snapped the knife closed in his palm.
See? he said, raising the closed knife
before my face, the green handle's
sheen beautiful and dangerous in
the dim light, and I began thinking
of the narrow spaces in our home
where such an object might be lost,
the lie I would have to tell to lose it.

Wild Fish

Snow on the high desert
crystallizes the second it lands
on the spiny heads of thistle,
the loose scrub brush—
or so it seemed to me
when I finally stopped after
a day's drive to the edge of a cliff
above the Deschutes where
my cousin lived and worked
at a state fish hatchery.
                              If you
could lift that snow, whole
and glistening like a sloughed skin,
it would rise in the vague shape
of the world. Ice as the memory
of water. It was hard to believe
that anything lived beneath
the surface of the still
reservoirs, though she told me
her hatchery was full of live things
as we walked along the troughs,
squinting.
                    Because it was time
and she wanted to surprise me
she threw a trowel-full of pellets
into the water, and the fish—
all of the fish in a ten-foot radius
flipped up with opened mouths,
flashing their slim, winter-silver
bodies in the unbroken air,
a visual applause.
                              Ecstatic
for a moment, then deeply
sad, then desperately weary, I
must have seemed deranged
to her. But she just handed me
the trowel, told me to try it, then

threw her arms around me,
said, *It'll get better.*
                    She'd divorced
that year, lost everything I was
losing but double: not
an apartment but a house, not
a lover but a husband, not
six years but twelve.
                    Indifferently,
the fish swam dark cursives
through the water until I
threw their food and they leaped—
not for joy as I would have
liked to believe. They were lovely
in their hunger. We toured
the property where I met
the trout, the Chinook salmon,
the great whiskered sturgeon
sitting in their man-made ponds
like weary oracles.
                    I tried
my best to keep up
with her long stride and talk
about how to tell the difference
between wild and domesticated
fish, how to raise a healthy breed.
I asked what kept the ospreys
from eating all the fish.
                    Nothing,
she said, shaking her head.
They'd tried nets above
the reservoirs, but the birds
got caught in them, polluted
whole populations with their deaths.
So the ospreys remain
consuming fish at random,
an incalculable loss. Some people want

dams, she told me, they want
industry—
               Some want only wild
fish in rivers untouched by
pollution. Still others want
to believe they can go on as
they have without attrition
of the land—that they can thrash
and harrow, but always wake
in the morning to find the lake
still there, the fish, consumed
the night before, miraculously
whole and alive in the water—
a child's dream.
               No. There is
always a reckoning. Even
my cousin, who loved
her husband right down
to his bones had to leave
when she saw, finally, what he was
doing, what he'd done all along.
One can live a lie for only so long.
We walked up the ridge, eroded
into smooth, straight edges, looked
down at the river gleaming
its promise, while I told her
how I'd been waiting
for the right time to leave, wanted
to find a way to go without
hurting him, though he'd hurt
me.
        I'd left him a letter, enough
money to fly home. I just
wanted to feel safe again and
for that to be all right. When I turned
the ignition key, a love song
blared from the radio

and for hours I drove, hardly seeing
where I swerved, terrified to leave,
still, more terrified to stay—
the way I'd grown accustomed to
living as if inside his dark throat.
When the sun set we walked
back to her house at the hatchery's
edge. She cooked and we stayed up
talking until my head felt
like a distant, buzzing
porch light.
            And that night
I dreamed of a fish who dreamed
of an osprey who swooped
down to clutch it, tear it
apart, but it strained
against his talons, made
his bird-heart beat so hard
that he dropped it
in the river, let it go.

Why I Left

After a while, surrender
resembles affection—the rust
on the wrought iron

grate flaking off a past
idea of love, or an old house
finally letting its eaves

sag toward the earth, crows
landing like old friends
in the brash, or that girl

in the dunes, half-covered
in sand with a dozen roses
of bullets across her chest:

how she lays there in welcome,
her arms splayed in the grit,
her face as blank as a white flag.

Cixous at the Café

If the autumn storm against the café window
is a woman's thighs, if the door opens
just as a grinder begins to scream,
if the rain wets the threshold darker,
foam floating on top of the coffee where

the coffee is everything & the foam
nothing, this false dichotomy perceivable
by the patrons, if the tenuous barista smiles
wearily as she plunges a spoon of sugar into
the cup, indicating her vacuous part in

a phallocentric language, waiting for the end
of her shift & a universal referent that might
include her, if the bell attached to the door
resonates & her boss says Hélène, pay attention,
as he wipes his thick hands on his apron,

smearing the white fabric with an unspoken
violence & later slips out of the bent metal
back door to smoke near the dumpsters, if
a feral black cat strides past him & before
he tries to speak, a shudder of humiliation

from his head to his pelvis loops through
his body like an electrical current, if he draws
his jacket tighter across his chest, unable
to vocalize his sudden lack, his throat closing
before he blacks out, falls to the pavement,

if the barista finds him, & recognizes his
affliction, calls an ambulance which arrives
with the connotation of emergency, but
the technicians can't, no matter how they
pound on his body, stabilize his pulse, or create

two equally positive & autonomous terms
for his & the barista's conditions, & if we
keep murmuring to one another as we stand in
the periphery, reenacting our role in the story,
& the structure that perpetuates the story—

Our Emotions Get Carried Away Beyond Us

When Pythagoras conceived of *the Music of the Spheres,* he believed he understood the universe—how celestial bodies moved in musical ratios—the world sensible and clean. This is why he lived simply, in the hills with his students, the mathematikoi, without need for possessions, women, or meat. The universe could be explained in rational signs,

so they drew equations and played instruments—not to please the gods, but to maintain their order in the universe. In the course of their practices, however, they found the proof of irrational numbers and concluded that the universe also contains things that are irrational. This idea so threatened the Pythagoreans that they kept its existence a secret.

When one of the students told an outsider about it, they drowned him in a lake. It's instinctive to be drawn toward water—thirst, baptism, a longing to be clean—so he would have thought nothing of following his friends, dust rising from the roads like a thin, glittering shroud. It was night but, because the day was hot, the water would have been as warm

as a body, like the summer waters of any dry landscape— eastern Oregon, even, with its bronzed hills, the air pungent with sage. I went there one summer with a friend I followed everywhere. She was a year older, lithe and electric, said she knew about men. We spent our days wandering whatever route led away from her family's cabin,

whatever cut through the knotweed and short, twisted pines, while I asked questions and she instructed, sometimes stopping in the shade of a boulder to practice kissing. *It hurts like this,* she said, touching my sunburned shoulders, *It always hurts like this*—until we grew weary, then wandered back. She also taught me how to measure the distance of lightning from earshot—

count the seconds between flash and thunder. Once, we were caught in a storm and ran home late, soaked, her mother and father already fighting by the time we arrived. Her mother burned the meat. He threw her by her shoulders to the floor, called her idiot, let his fist hang over her, white as a star. And by daylight, the women with their coolers by the river,

over their minted cigarettes and Solo cups full of gin, squinted toward their children wading in the water, talked about the latest news: a woman who, sick of loneliness, drowned her children for the man she loved. They shook their heads—a slow, uncertain no—and sipped until the faint glow of their smokes lit intermittently in the darkness, a code.

Years later when trying to leave a brutal lover, I would return to him crying and he would bite into my shoulder, leave a plum-colored crescent, and I'd think of those women—of how we deserved it. *It hurts. It always hurts like this,* my friend murmured to me in shade or in darkness. But each morning when we left the cabin, when the sun slanted toward us (too-bright arrows),

we were silent as we aimed for the old, familiar trail, silent as we wandered away from the path, each other, to walk figure-eights in the wild scrub brush, listen to the patterns of the wind. We like to say *the song of the wind,* but if there is a song it offers no meaning, no explanation, only a music we can't order, or else an order that's always undone by what we don't yet perceive.

So, no perfect music as the *mathematikoi* believed. Only the few notes Pythagoras must have hummed to himself as he walked back beneath the erratic stars, his sleeves and hem still wet from the lake. Only his voice wavering above a rhythm of footsteps as he wove between the dark arms of juniper, while the boy's eyes beneath the water, no longer seeing, remained open.

In, Out

Clouds pull loose and the sun glints through
a window exposing the architecture
of the air—beams of swirling dust buttressed
by shadow and a girl who spins through them,

bright and dark at once. She is not working,
only whirling and we can't know what she is
in her mind—a dancer, an unhinged gyre, cream
being whipped into butter. We can't know

because she hasn't decided. The propellers
she imagines her arms make, break through
the beams, the dust spiraling away from her
body and toward her body because when

we spin, the air spins with us. Think of a turbine
breathing out smoke, the smoke rolling toward
and away the way it must have when Pompeii
was earthed, the ash rushing in and rushing out.

There must have been a girl twirling in a room,
her mother at the doorway waiting for a man
to return to them, ultimately returning
in smoke. As she turned beneath the arch,

shocked, amidst the iridescent air, she must
have realized that it was always this way
in her mind. She was always just about to turn
toward the girl to begin their lives. Did I say

the architecture of air? I meant to say: The spaces
that contain us. I meant to say: *Stop your spinning,
girl, look out*—but it was already too late for
that girl that I was, reeling as the ash rushed in.

American Fable

The world is flat, and you've arrived
in the far west corner, where the plateau
you've been discovering drops into
the lovely black of space. Your gods
form the delicate chain of constellation
you are guided by and here they are
close enough to touch. A powerful
musk has sunk between your fingers
from tangling your hands in the hair
of the beast that brought you here—
a bison cow, kneeling now, in her
weariness and knowing, as in winter
when one is separated from the herd
by wolves, and knows to lay down.
You never thought you'd see the end,
or that the end would be so stunning:
small, bright meteors falling almost
into your hands, near your rough cheek,
past your ears like fireflies on the plains
of your childhood. You invent a jar
to capture them in—a way to keep them
falling infinitely toward you without
burning out. You feel a song whelming
in your throat as the sky turns crucible,
as the ether hums with the golden light
of your making. Too bad there is no one
to share in your delight. Only the dusky
savages watch in the brush. Like wind
they rise with fury, settle into a hush.

A Dream of Water

I'd walked a long way through warm rain
from the party I'd left drunk to get more liquor,
linked with a stranger who said he knew
the way, but then forgot the way, led me down
street after street, past lonely soccer fields,
past the abandoned bread factory, a house
with a tense, gray pit-bull chained to an elm,
its branches reaching over him like great, rough
hands—
        how the stranger paused to taunt her,
to call her *baby* and *honey* as if they were lovers,
to make me laugh, which I did—everything
was funny then, the way the air spun, the way
the stranger's handsome face sharpened
and shifted in the streetlight, the dog's
snarls veering into shrieks as he twirled me
away from the fence into a broken waltz,
whispering *she's just jealous* into my ear, his
hand gripping my wrist too tightly, leading me
out of the light.
        Where are we going? I asked,
stumbling because he was pulling me
ahead toward an empty space at the end
of the road. The smell of exhaust and muddy
water made me realize we were at the dark
slipping edge of the river. I laughed out
and the laugh bounced off the concrete
into the water, and knew if I didn't follow
I'd die, so I did.
        I snapped away from him,
pounding into the water, the cold of it
shocking the breath almost out of me.
I beat and glided, shedding my shoes
as I went, my soaked jeans sinking away
as I dove out of sight, curled up in
the currents sweeping me away.
When I breached, I drew one long breath

then dove again. It was like that a while:
swimming down to hide, swimming up
to breathe, my wet body a slender needle
in the fabric of the river.
                            Even when
I knew I'd gone too far, I swam out farther,
became lighter, my nerves untangling in
the bright flashes that sometimes shone
on the water—bridge lights overhead.
The drift carried me downstream, my breath
regular, my heart beating. After a while,
I turned onto my back to look at the stars,
let my legs float up, the gleam of my toes
on the water, aquatic flowers. By the time
I reached the gritty shore, miles downstream,
pulled myself out of the river, I'd already
decided not to tell anyone. I let the story
roll down my shoulders on my cool walk
back, become a dream I once had of water.

Jung at the Harbor

The tide is a kind of alchemy on the shore—
a dream that dreams
itself. Far away in the desert

there's a man who can listen to
the rhythm of the earth, or believes he can
which, in the end, is the same thing

since the mind can contain everything
past and future—but Jung wonders
what it sounds like—the high-pitched

keening of nerves? The lowly, repeating
thud of the heart? In the distance
a ship moans into the edgeless ocean—

what is it, if not desire? He's lost
his mind, and has come here to find it.
He builds little castles from the loose rock,

making sure the structures are balanced.
At home, the archetype of wives
prepares his evening meal. As she lifts

the kettle and ladles the soup in bowls,
he cups his hands to the water. This synchronicity
is marriage. An unconscious

lulling together like the endless span
of the horizon and the ship moving away
out of distinct view until it becomes

part of the collective memory of ships,
and part of his memory, where it continues
its journey further and further in

the horizon of his mind, so that he no longer
knows it. He traveled on a ship like that once.
Part of him departed here. Look: the waves.

Spring

Silly green-aired tornado
swooning like an assassin
in love with its mark, the land—

the callused fingered land,
the big-eyed land
with its muscly shoulders

and a blank stare you can
sow anything into—
Oh, and the silos filled with grain.

Oh, and the air, allowing anything
in, lonely widow opening
her screen door for the salesman

with his toxins in bottles,
evaporates ready for
uncorking. *Yes*, she says, *open them all.*

They build a bonfire in her
living room, throwing the earth
in to watch it transform

into ash, to drift up into
cumulus, the rain, the green sky
twisting itself into a scream

while we wait in the cellar
huddled together, praying
that love will not find us.

Blackout

There is nothing electric to make us ascend
the side of the building, no light to reach us
up here, where we are stuck in the invisible

elevator between desert and sky, our bodies
distilled—*spirits* because what we drink is
the ghost of the grain in the field. Moonlight

throws gloss on the crowd below, their faces
skyward (toward what? an answer?). We sense
the earth releasing its heat, the churn of insects

out in the dunes, that writhing—

———————

In this dim nocturnal world we're uncertain
of ourselves, could become anything now, become
each other, flesh-colored insects
in the deep Mojave,

burrowing down. *What are they called?*

Children of the Earth, a woman's voice says
(in a Spanish accent), her hair a burnt-star black.

Where are we? Someone asks. We see only shadow
selves. Perhaps this is the abyss we've been

slated for. *Maybe we're dead*, someone says,
maybe me.
        No, another voice rises—

       We're too high up.

———————

Further out, past the unlit neon and crowds
of Joshua trees, a wall of concrete
once applauded
                    by floodlights rises out of the thin
                    desert river. We begin

to mistake the river
for currents of memory, the dam for the doors
that won't open.

                    The darkness is a net that pulls
                    us together. *What*

does it matter if we never remember ourselves
as ourselves?

                    It doesn't.

——————

Somewhere there's sunlight
tumbling out of doors refracting through windows, loose

in the fine strands of a woman's hair. Somewhere there's something
to hide from. But here we unfurl—

fronds in a vascular dark—no longer hold ourselves
accountable, no longer
                    apologize for the lack

of space. We don't remember
who we were
before—*Is this Union? Is this Love?* Someone sings
one long note
                    and it fills our chests, our throats

the closed room, the street below us, like smoke, like roots
spreading, we are almost completely—

Remedy

The bone has grown back now. The girl
runs her fingers along the tops of hedges,
stone walls, the oily-smooth surfaces of sills,
the bald, shallow impression in her skull where
the burr hole was drilled, where her hair
will never grow back. The rest of her hair
is long and black. She lets it fall to one side,
over her shoulder because it covers the spot

and because she is taller, the bones in her face
sharper, her hips widening, the architecture
of her shape studied by men. When she visits
the doctors with their cold metal instruments
and feels the rough paper dress against her skin,
she blushes. When she paints her toenails,
her knees drawn up against her chest, she lets
her eyes flicker over the tiny red splashes

and barely recalls a cluster of scenes: her body
trembling without her, the swirling, too-bright
room, the pointed white of the hospital, her
own voice vibrating in her throat like a strange
bird caught there, wing-clipped and thrashing,
a terrible ache that she no longer remembers,
only that it was there inside her skull, a great
crushing pain. Then she opened her eyes

underwater, in a deep trench of sleep where
phosphorescent fish bumped against her head
clamped in place by a large vice as the surgeons
drilled the hole into her skull. They didn't know
why her brain swelled, only that she'd brought
them to the end of their knowledge, this the only
course for keeping her alive: a hole in the head.
She felt the fish swim away, a powerful current
rushing out of her—

Days stretch out now with nothing in them,
her adolescent summers like bleached sheets
hanging on the line. She wonders if this is
what it is to be a woman; her body mutinous,
burrowed into. Moths beat wildly at her smudged
window and she closes her eyes, too tired to
watch them suffer. She runs her fingers along
countertops, the edges of unopened books, slowly,

because she has nothing to hurry toward. She is
waiting, she thinks, for someone to heal her.
It makes her angry, but she doesn't know why.
Her shoulders tighten. Sweat beads at her hairline,
rolls down her face. She imagines herself as
a flower deep in a swamp, which, once found,
will be ground into paste, rubbed into the body
of a fevered stranger, used as a cure for pain.

After Fever

I'm too far from the pain now
to still call it mine. It's someone else's pain—

blood bright on a horse's neck after a fly ascends
from his body, the pasture. The horse turns

his ears toward the wind. His large eyes
are black, which is different from darkness.

I never hid there, in the eyes of that horse.
That horse never kept my knife

by his side, and the pain it promised
to free me from no longer keeps me

as its own. I can tell you now, because those
who might call themselves witness

question their stories. They murmur
in their sleep. They forget the sun-stroke summer,

the scything rain, and now it's been so long
I too forget. See how the live oaks no longer

thrash themselves? See how the moon no longer
stalks the sky? Sometimes I fall asleep without

closing my eyes—my lover's thumb
a talisman in my fist, my face pressed to his back

as if into the spine of an open book, the words
almost reading themselves. I walk hypnotic through

fields, touch the loose grasses, the flecked silt
shoulders of the floodless delta. I turn

my ear toward the stone. It's almost
as if my heart never stopped, as if a weight never

smothered me down. It's as if that knife never sung
in my skin, as if there never was a fever to break.

How the Soul Discharges its Emotions
Against False Objects

The blind hallucinate. In a story I heard on the radio, one blind man could hear his eyes singing to him. I was driving and pulled over to listen. The guest neurologist explained that the brain is a glutton for sensation—when one sense goes out, the brain turns on itself, just as it does when a limb is severed, and haunts the site of its severing—*phantom pain*. Loss also causes hallucination:

The Pythia of Delphi each lost their names, their bodies, before they were worthy of Apollo's breath. Some say the volcanic pneuma beneath the shrine, built at the axis of two fault lines, caused their oracular hallucinations. Some say they could speak the god's chaotic will because they were pure, they were lonely. The radio show ended and I pulled onto the road, the name

of the street as blank inside me as my knowledge of the engine beneath the hood of my car, that richly-oiled machine fretting against its own parts. On a billboard above me, there was an image from the Pompeii exhibit on display in the city museum: a human form, thrown down by the weight of ash, faceless, details erased, a solid, untranslated secret. Sometimes I hold the box

of old letters I found written in code, a cipher I invented with a girlhood friend to conceal our secrets, though I can no longer read the symbols and that girl whose hair once fell across my face is lost. There's no one left to utter the signs, no priests to mediate the meaning. As a child I was always a passenger, left to watch the grey city shifting around me without any knowledge

of where I was led. At intersections, I'd look into the windows of other cars, wonder where they were going, why I didn't know who they were, though they looked familiar, though I might have mistaken them for someone I knew, like Mrs. Blue, who, after her husband's death called each passerby by her husband's name. He was stabbed by a thief in their front garden and lay down in the cool, loose earth. She'd lived with him sixty years, and in the months between his death and hers, she wandered through our yards in her wrinkled dress, weeping on our porches, already a ghost. Everyone shook their heads in pity, though no one opened their doors to her because that kind of grief is contagious. I never saw her after she died. I don't have that gift,

that curse. But that winter I had a fever so high it made the walls shimmer their terrible light, the floors buzz with longing. I felt the earth's breath possess me, let me see through its surface, and even after the fever broke, for months I was haunted by the shapes inside it: mandala, uroboros, spiral, eye, everything shifting beneath the stunted veneer of sight—what Cassandra must have

seen the moment she tried to rise from Apollo, who only wanted her again and again—it was too much. Some say when she refused to sate him, he scorned her, made everyone think she was insane, as if, otherwise, everyone would have listened. That onerous vision of an army in the belly of a horse—who would have believed it wasn't a symbol, a sickness in her, but a gift on the eve of a fall?

Subplot

We're stunned to have awakened
from the bright illusion
to discover our lives

ordinary—the cups in the cupboards
static and clean, refusing to tremble
with light. We're stunned

to realize that we have spoken
the few lines given to us,
that we didn't say them so valiantly

as we had imagined, and now we can't
edit, can't inhale again the last
halo of smoke, can't leap

from the train to land
in other cities, other lives
that had been, all along, waiting

for us to arrive. Our animals
whimper at their empty bowls.
Our lovers wake up in our arms,

already exhausted by daylight
from which we can't save them.
We have too much to do.

After work, we'll go to a movie
to sit in the dark, contemplate
the shifting screen, light—clips of wind

and overexposed cirrus, ice
from a glacial field, a sudden kiss, a body
falling and falling, something

that resembles a story which resembles
all other stories. Eventually, we'll exit
the black parentheses of the theatre, drive

toward home, where we will relinquish
our keys to the dim hallway—the clink
reverberating as we walk to our beds

apprising the horizon where the sun
has already set and a cast of city lights
will applaud themselves until dawn.

The Physicists

Who is to say, now, we ever went to Spain where the ciders
are more sour than sweet, where we followed

a night parade in the street, the drums and spinning torches,
the people whose faces blurred in the barely there
light and shadow. Now time makes them

impossible to see clearly. Now they are only a blur of human
forms, as indistinct as the voices that rose

from the cobblestone calling us down
and out and away. We loved each other once.
How unremarkably the street lamps shone that night,

how unspecific the music that we were certain
was a sign. When we arrived in the plazuela

it was midnight and a bonfire glowed
on everyone's faces—everyone who was called,
or so they believed, by the burning drums

the dancers' rough pirouettes, the thrill of not knowing
where we were led. No one can see

the black holes they tell us are spinning in space
with the earthly eye, but we believe
they swallow everything and beyond

the laws of physics which tell us nothing
disappears—there is only altering, transformation—

even the physicists are afraid that, when those dead
stars stop spinning everything they drew
into them will cease to exist. We circled the bonfire

dizzy with cider, the way cinders amplify the night until
the parade broke up and without knowing why

we stopped dancing, turned back to our rooms—
our room where, some nights when I drew the wooden
shutters, the air was so still, so dark.

After the Divorce

I knew if I began with a bird then
it would have to fly away at the end
so instead I placed a stone in your
palm the one I'd worn smooth with
my tongue it took years though you
never thought to ask how I made it
and I don't ask about the green bird
building a nest in your other palm
though I know it must be a gift from
a lover and I am sundered when it sings

Freud at the Laundromat

a circle that turns within a box and slots
where the money goes and goes transparent
door that opens to anonymous red panties

oh if only undergarments could speak he'd
analyze the fuck out of them but suffices
with pressing his ear to each hot door trying

to hold still long enough to memorize the
cadence of zippers slapping steel the little
hooks of bras and the top seams of dresses

tapping lightly in the load sweat glossing
his forehead where he was supposed to be
he can't remember perhaps he's had too much

cocaine tonight it's winter in Vienna he blinks
out to the woolen sky, white drifts and fog
repressing his view of the street a hazy lamp

penetrates the darkness the sores in his mouth
must be cut out again and he dreams of his wife's
younger sister *Minna, Minna* and their apartment

at 19 Berggasse—the lie they conceived that
also had to be cut out oh now he is too old
his penis alone in his grey, wrinkled slacks

he wants to take them off, throw them in with
. a stranger's clothes watch the legs wrap around
the other unfilled pants a psychosomatic twitch

controls his left wrist he clears his throat again
again what will it take to be rid of this constant
vertigo aching he imagines that death is like

a long dose of morphine but is still terrified
oh to awaken inside another body perhaps be
the child Minna canceled this time around kept

Zoo

A lone silverback squatted at the edge
of the man-made ravine, opposite the side where I stood,
watching him watch me—his thick torso

twisted away. I knew enough not
to stare too long, glanced down to show him I meant
no harm. He began pissing, looking

right at me, as if to say, *Fuck you
for wanting to see this.* In the Night Hunter's Auditorium
the aardvarks were more gregarious, clambering

over each other like circus clowns to get to
the processed termites near the window, where

although they didn't look my way, one beast tried
to hump the other while she ate, climbing up
onto her haunches and biting her long slender ears.

They were calamitous lovemakers,
there, in the gloaming, him trying to mount her,

her kicking him away with her
mouth full of grubs, which I imagine
are bitter, intestinal, but perhaps I'm wrong.

Perhaps this was as good as it gets for an aardvark.
Interpretation is always symbolic

of one's own mind which is why
the *Bubo virginianus*—a North American owl, too large
for her exhibition cage—just enough room

to jump-flap her way to a single synthetic oak limb,
then hop down again—seemed perpetually surprised
at my presence, as if I'd parachuted into the gray, dim-lit

hallway as an anomalous species—one of those rare
upright gorillas who might recognize herself

in the glass—that reflection in the cage like another,
transparent self with a plastic branch growing
from her chest, a mural of clouds drifting through

her head—one who isn't fooled by the mural's ruse
of sky. One who knows better than to be there.

We Are Bored

So we line our bottles on the fence and aim, or swim
into the river's gullet, let it swallow us bare—the vellum
sheen of mud on our skin. We drive for hours into
the wind, chasing last light and a time before toil, stage
a breakdown, strike a flare just to see who pulls over.
We blindfold and spin each other around, assault piñatas
with blunt sticks, heat the flesh of a hog in a pit—
charcoal and dirt—until we can pull its eyes from its face.
We get so lit we stagger across the sky. We burn
our cigars, the dense scent of burning loam sucked
down our throats, our lungs shuddering like dying
birds, or we trace our shadows, punch the air, rub
welts into each other's arms, pull off our clothes,
climb into back seats, press our mouths against windows
to write our names on glass. We pluck the bright faces
of flowers, stick our fists into hives to steal the afterglow.
We build forts from bed sheets to hide in, kiss, slap each
other's faces, tour the periphery of abandoned buildings.
We follow the sound of sirens away from the suburbs
into the thrumming cities, crowd on the sidewalks to
watch medics pulling the bodies away. We dare each other
into graveyards to fuck against tombstones, walk out
into traffic, change our names, quit our jobs, migrate
to other cities, tattoo ourselves with the names of lovers
who will try to forget us. We jump out of airplanes,
earth as open as an eye as we fall irrevocably toward it.
We pound our fists on the hoods of cars, stare into
the blazing fires we've set, light dynamite in the open fields
just to see how fast we can run. We wrestle with the ghosts
of our fathers, look so long at constellations we see
our faces in them. We break into factories, winnow
crowbars into the turbines, throw bricks through the sooted
windows, set the goddamn things on fire. We rush into
the revival tent to swoon into salvation, handle the serpents,
prove we are pure, we are holy. We talk in tongues, pierce

our nipples, drive ink-guns into our shoulders, slam a bat
into the clerk's face, gamble the house away, give our money
to God, incite riots we have no intention of stopping, rev
our engines at stoplights, drag razors over the soft inside
of thighs, sink into bathtubs, kneel in pews, kneel in alleys,
kneel closed-eyed on the filthy mattress, light the pipe,
lie to our families, invent past lovers, divorce our wives
just to marry them again, denounce our children,
then ask their forgiveness. We dance wildly in the arms
of strangers, swallow another handful of pills, throw
a wedding party where the groom is unfettered and where,
already, the bride is crying. We drink champagne and eat
our cake too, throw a ball into the grandstand, roll a joint,
spike the punch, conceive a child who will hate us.
We write poems, run red lights, get so lost in the forest
we nearly starve. We go to the office with three shotguns
and a bomb. We look for weapons of mass destruction,
confess to prostitutes, tell stories to lawyers. We swallow
amphetamines to work through the night, go into
the mountains to learn from the sky. We run for no reason
in the split-light morning, go down to the jail to steal
the prisoners, hang them from sycamores, telephone polls.
We stab a flag into the chest of the moon, keep watching
the screen though it only shows static. We march through
the streets to show our medals, toss up confetti, pitch
hard candies at children, we beat our drums, shine our
trumpets, twirl batons so high they seem to matter, walk
deep into the desert to watch the bomb go off, to watch it
grow and grow like a backwards cloud rooted from dunes.
We speculate on how we can use it: for love, entertainment,
profit, the poor. We can use it to prove our strength, use it
for the war we never want to end, the war we keep starting,
the unkempt war with its mouth gaping, with its fists against
the caves like a monstrous, vacant child, the sun cracking
our skin, the sandstorms blasting our faces open. We let

the heat wilt our minds as we wander back into the suburbs,
beneath the wan streetlights, beyond the cul-de-sac's end.
We whittle our names into the trunks of pines, which harrow
us with the way they stand so still under the sun and rain,
never feeling the slow rot of the heart, never waking to
the light of their failures, never lying down across the steel
rails of the trellis the way we do just to feel the weight of
the iron beneath us, the damp air rising up from the river
through the blank, splintered wood, and that long, slow
moan deep in our bones—the call of the oncoming train.

Fire Map

The dry summer hills of the West are
         devoured, again, by smoke—brocaded
                  black char in the arcs of trees,
and fire still rising, moving

         faster—helicopters whipping
overhead to drop young men
                  with axes and shovels

to extinguish the flames before they reach
         the county tinderbox. I took
                  a man home with me once,
         years ago—one who claimed he could

skydive into crisis. It was winter,
         the off-season. We sat in a dim
bar in Los Angeles, drinking

         ember-colored whiskey until,
                  heartbroken and reckless, I wanted
         to know how hard he could land
on my body, how his scars might rise

         fresh beneath my fingers
                  but he shocked me most
                  by how softly he kissed, the lines
in his face drawn deeper, how he fell

         asleep fully clothed and curled up
against me like a hurt child. He left
         that night, so I saw him last
in silhouette, the city flickering
         behind him, farther and farther out—

This morning, I hear
        eleven Hotshots have died since
the wildfires began. As far as I know
        he's still inside the inferno

with a fire map folded
        in his pocket to know where
            to fight, how to find
        his way back: flames drawn

across a worried topography—red
        where the intensity is greatest,
            arrows divining the fire's path
        fed by wind, marking where
            he must dig his trench straight
                down to rock

where nothing burns,
            where layers of bone,
        loam, and dust have been pressed
            by time into something beyond
            destruction.

After the Twentieth Century

For a while now, there's been a pain in
my chest on the side where my heart isn't.
Winter came and went, trying to numb,
but now the spring trees are at it again,

wasting the seeds and fine dust of their longings
on windshields, the grooves of sidewalks,
the faces of dispassionate drivers. I'm not
interested in anatomy, or the nuances of deciduous

courtship, or even how I woke this morning
after a night of strange dreams: a girl alone
on the metro, who looked suspiciously
like me, who brushed her thin brown hair

gently, until it pulled loosed from her scalp.
And her eyes, when she saw the little nests
of hair in her palms, looked sad, but unalarmed—
gray saltwater caught in a bay, wearing down

the gritty embankment, the bridges, rolling pebbles
smooth, not because it has to, but because it
doesn't know what else to do. What else to do
but ebb and flow, follow a shoreline, fill a space

in the body of the earth? When I woke, it was
raining—the sky a thin pour of whiskey.
In the courtyard of clotheslines a white sheet hung,
soaked through like belief, that trick of desire.

On Prognostications

Still, the attempt persists: to read the sky as we might a book, or scattered runes on the floor of an approaching disaster. Disaster, from the Greek, meaning "bad star." *In the atmosphere, there are bowls with the hollow side turned toward us, in which the bright vapors are collected to produce flames, which are the heavenly bodies*, an ancient scholar writes of the credos of Heraclitus. All those dense planets

and meteors spinning in their lonely orbits out in the black cold. All the people on earth walking into and out of umbra, unaware of the tumors swelling inside them. Whole cosmos of cells. If only they'd think to look up or go to their physicians, who can peer inside them, divine a forecast from their inner constellations. Cancer settled for the second time in the breast

of a friend who died in autumn. She heeded all warnings, suffered radiation, surgery, chemo, but at every stage the doctors gave a new prognosis: *good*, then *poor*, then *it's unlikely she'll live to the New Year*. She was an atheist, who sang in a choir because she liked the vibrations of music in her throat, because she wanted to create something beautiful in the world, however fleeting.

Even now, in 2014, voices arise through the electric atmosphere, insisting the tetrad of lunar eclipses are blood moons of biblical prophesy. And there are people in the world who claim magic cures. At the century's turn, I traveled to a shaman who lived on the periphery of Cape Town. Splintered wood islands lay purposefully in the dirt floor of his healing theater. Elements of his craft swayed lightly on twine clouds hung from the ceiling's

exposed rafters: blackened honeycomb, nests of thorns, dried birds feet and bones, skins of animals, and a single gold watch like a pendulum at the center of the room. All along his shelves were powders and dusty vodka bottles filled with liquids of orange or green, or empty. He led me through his menagerie, explaining that cancer was a hex he could fix like all

ailments of witchcraft. He pointed to a bottle he told me cures
colic, another an antidote for kidney and back pain, the third a
remedy for anything and everything: *If this does not cure you, you
are hopeless*. I told him nothing was wrong with me. He laughed
replied, *Nothing you know of yet*. In the years after the buildings
fell, in the airports of New York and DC, I often heard a calm,

disembodied voice floating over the crowds of passengers on their
paths toward their terminals: *Code Orange*, meaning increased
security, random arrests, the irradiating of each body before it
flew from the earth. Comets in reverse. Bad stars. Dark matter
spreading the universe wider, growing in all of us. The last time
I pressed my friend's hand in mine it felt like the page

of a new book, so light and cool, then she looked straight at me
when she said, without longing or spite, "Have a happy life."
That was her way: always looking directly, even if into a wound,
a void. In one distant fragment, Heraclitus writes, *A road up and
down are one and the same*. Sometimes I dream of the moment
she died, when she left her body like a chorus.

The Needle, The Thread

What am I suppose
        to do with all of this
happiness? The needle

that pierced through
        then the thread that
follows, that seems

immeasurable, but so
        thin, delicate. I run
my fingers along

the healed seams
        in my skin, the patched
ruptures in the walls

of my mind. But now
        the storm has washed
the pavement, lost water

rises from its unadorned
        body and the flowering
trees flood the gutters

with pink. What am I
        supposed to do with
the scent of the weeds,

the sharp, impatient
        greenness of them, split,
as I am, with a history

of sorrow? When I breathe
        the sweet June light, my
lungs crackle, my hair

stands on end. What do
    I do with this swirl of
pines, the wasp nest's

astonishing swell, the rifts
    in the maple, rough
beneath my hands,

and my God, the sky—
    the sky—

Notes

The following titles were borrowed from the titles of essays by Michel de Montaigne, translated by M.A. Screech: "We Can Savor Nothing Pure," "On the Uncertainty of Our Judgment," "To Philosophize is to Learn to Die," "Our Emotions Get Carried Away Beyond Us," "How the Soul Discharges its Emotions Against False Objects," "On Prognostications."

Dirge with a Love Song in it
For my grandmother, Mary Steinmuller (Campillo).

American Libretto
All quotes in this poem are taken from section 276 of *The Gay Science* by Friedrich Nietzsche.

On the Uncertainty of Our Judgment
For John Cranley, Cincinnati's 69th Mayor, who, since taking office in 2013, has laughed his way through at least two damaging spills (fracking chemical and oil) in the Ohio River, from which the city's residents draw their drinking water.

To Philosophize is to Learn to Die
This poem makes reference to the victims of the December 14, 2012 Sandy Hook Elementary School shooting in Newtown, Connecticut. I find it enraging and profoundly sad that there have been so many such tragedies in our country that I would have to explain which one I meant.

Constellation
For Melissa.

Cixous at the Café
Écriture feminine, literally translated to "women's writing," is a term first coined by French feminist literary theorist Hélène Cixous in her essay, "The Laugh of the Medusa" (1975). The term

was often used by French feminists who focused their analyses on the inscription of the female body and female difference in language. That is, the way language constructs and maintains a hierarchical order of patriarchal meaning.

On Prognostications
For my friend, Cathryn Long.
The opening italicized quote was taken from the works of Diogenes Laertius, the second from the works of Hippolytus, both quoted in *The Texts of Early Greek Philosophers: The Complete Fragments and Selected Testimonies of the Major Presocratics*, part 1, translated and edited by Daniel W. Graham.

Acknowledgments

Thank you to Denise Duhamel for choosing this collection for the
Barrow Street Book Contest. Thank you to Barrow Street Books,
and especially my editor, Peter Covino, for publishing this collection.
Thank you to the Ohio Arts Council for their Individual Excellence
Award and to the Charles Phelps Taft Research Center their
Summer Research Fellowship, both of which have allowed me to
finish this collection.

Sincere thanks to the editors of the following journals and
anthologies in which these poems first appeared, sometimes
under different titles:

After Montaigne (U. of Georgia Press): "How the Soul Discharges
    its Emotions Against False Objects."
Arts & Letters: "Subplot" and "Somewhere Always Fire."
Basalt: "The Physicists."
Crazyhorse: "The Needle, The Thread."
Diagram: "Our Emotions Get Carried Away Beyond Us" and
    "To Philosophize is to Learn How to Die."
Fugue: "Constellation" (previously "A Romance").
Global Poetry Anthology: the 2013 Montreal International
    Poetry Prize by Véhicule Press: "Transit."
Hayden's Ferry Review: "The End of Fathers."
Hotel Amerika: "We Can Savor Nothing Pure."
Locuspoint: "American Fable" (previously "Cowboy").
Nimrod: "Burning House."
North American Review: "Zoo" (previously "At the Zoo").
Smartish Pace: "Jung at the Harbor."
The Journal: "Winter Inversion."
The Kenyon Review (KROnline): "We Are Bored" and "American
    Curse."
The Laurel Review: "On Prognostications."
The Missouri Review: "After the Twentieth Century," "Revolution,"
    and "Lacan at the Carousel."

Thank you to Sow's Ear Press for publishing my chapbook, *American Libretto*, as an issue of their journal in which the following poems appeared: "After the Twentieth Century," "We Can Savor Nothing Pure," "Burning House," "American Libretto," "Lacan at the Carousel," "To Philosophize is to Learn How to Die," "After the Revolution," "Somewhere Always Fire," "Interrogator's Love Letter," "Our Emotions Get Carried Away Beyond Us," "Zoo," "Jung at the Harbor," "The End of Fathers," "How the Soul Discharges its Emotions Against False Objects," "The Physicists," "Transit," "American Curse," and "We Are Bored."

Thank you to Toph Woodward for always being my first and last reader: without your friendship, my life and work would be rather confusing and sad. Thank you also to Shara Lessley, Dana Levin, Lindsay Bernal, Brian Brodeur and Steve Roberts who've given me valuable feedback at various stages of this manuscript. To the Luscious Ladies of Letters (Jennifer Malat, Nicole Starosielski, and Eva Hayward) who literally sat with me and encouraged me while I wrote this book: a million thanks and much love. Thank you to all those at the University of Cincinnati English department for allowing me pre-tenure leave to finish this collection, and especially five colleagues, Leah Stewart, Don Bogen, John Drury, Jay Twomey, and Christine Mok, for your encouragement and support. Thank you also to my beloved poetry professors, Jacqueline Osherow and Katharine Coles, at the University of Utah where several of these poems were first written and read.

Thank you to five wonderful people, April Wilder, Natanya Pulley, Vincent Caruso, Elijah Millgram, and Max Stinson, all of whom gave me a home and a place to write during what otherwise would have been a homeless year. And special thanks to Max, my love, with whom I now share a home permanently, and to our son, Mercer, for making the world brighter.

Danielle Cadena Deulen's previously published books include a collection of poems *Lovely Asunder* (U. of Arkansas Press, 2011), which won the Miller Williams Arkansas Poetry Prize and the Utah Book Award; and a memoir, *The Riots* (U. of Georgia Press, 2011), which won the AWP Prize in Creative Nonfiction and the GLCA New Writers Award. She has been the recipient of a Jay C. and Ruth Halls Poetry Fellowship from the University of Wisconsin-Madison and an Ohio Arts Council Individual Excellence Award. Danielle lives with her family in Salem, Oregon where she teaches in the English Department at Willamette University.

BARROW STREET POETRY

Our Emotions Get Carried Away Beyond Us
Danielle Cadena Deulen (2015)

Radioland
Lesley Wheeler (2015)

Tributary
Kevin McLellan (2015)

Horse Medicine
Doug Anderson (2015)

This Version of Earth
Soraya Shalforoosh (2014)

Unions
Alfred Corn (2014)

O, Heart
Claudia Keelan (2014)

Last Psalm at Sea Level
Meg Day (2014)

Vestigial
Page Hill Starzinger (2013)

You Have to Laugh: New + Selected Poems
Mairéad Byrne (2013)

Wreck Me
Sally Ball (2013)

Blight, Blight, Blight, Ray of Hope
Frank Montesonti (2012)

Self-evident
Scott Hightower (2012)

Emblem
Richard Hoffman (2011)

Mechanical Fireflies
Doug Ramspeck (2011)

Warranty in Zulu
Matthew Gavin Frank (2010)

Heterotopia
Lesley Wheeler (2010)

This Noisy Egg
Nicole Walker (2010)

Black Leapt In
Chris Forhan (2009)

Boy with Flowers
Ely Shipley (2008)

Gold Star Road
Richard Hoffman (2007)

Hidden Sequel
Stan Sanvel Rubin (2006)

Annus Mirabilis
Sally Ball (2005)

A Hat on the Bed
Christine Scanlon (2004)

Hiatus
Evelyn Reilly (2004)

3.14159+
Lois Hirshkowitz (2004)

Selah
Joshua Corey (2003)